E
Spotter Jotter

This Aircraft Spotter Jotter belongs to:	
Telephone Number:	
Spotter Jotter Book Number:	

From: Day	Date	Month	Year
To: Day	Date	Month	Year

Above: Flybe operated Embraer ERJ-175STD, registration G-FBJA, on final approach to Manchester International Airport on 24/11/13.
Cover Photo: Monarch operated Airbus A321-231, registration G-ZBAM, taxis into Manchester International Airport on 5/7/14.
Upper Back Cover: EasyJet operated Airbus A319-111, registration, G-EZDR "Keri Emerton", taxis into Manchester International Airport on 5/7/14.
Middle Cover: KLM operated Boeing 737, registration PH-BGK departs Manchester International Airport on 13/4/13.
Lower Back Cover: Emirates operated Airbus A380-861, registration A6-EDM, begins its journey from Manchester International Airport on 5/7/14.

Safety First

Fortunately the UK generally tolerates what some may class as the eccentric behaviour of people wanting to spot and photograph aircraft. Unfortunately, this is not the same in some other countries though, so if travelling abroad to pursue your hobby, check to see what is accepted first.

Whilst you can spot and photograph aircraft in the UK, with the current terrorism threat we now all face around the world you still need to be sensible how you go about your hobby. By following the points below you will keep yourself and others safe and be allowed to enjoy your hobby without issue.

Passenger at the Airport

Years ago, most airports had viewing platforms where you could go see and photograph aircraft moving about the aprons. However, these days this opportunity is quite rare and you are more likely to be looking at aircraft through the glass windows of the departure lounge. If you do want to spot or take photographs, please follow the points below:

- Be courteous to others and don't get in the way of passengers or staff, especially, if your are in transit from one place to another.
- Do not use "selfy sticks".
- Do not use flash photography. Turn your flash off.
- Do not be tempted to photograph the airport interior.
- Do not enter into areas passengers cannot go into unless you have permission to do so.
- If challenged, be polite and do what is asked.
- Walk, don't run.
- Make sure you keep you possessions with you at all times.
- No hi-jinx or rowdy behaviour, no matter how excited you are to get that elusive spot!

At the Airport – Visitor

If you have been granted permission to visit an airport or airfield, please follow the points below:

- Follow the instructions of your host. The instructions are for your safety and the safety of the airport.
- If you have been granted permission to go airside, you and your camera bag etc will be subjected to a security check first. It would be prudent to check before hand that you do not have any dangerous or sharp objects with you, like mini-screwdrivers or camera lens cleaning fluid.
- Wear Personal Protective Equipment as required or as provided.
- Stick to marked walking routes and do not take short cuts. Never approach aircraft unless you have permission to do so or are accompanied.
- Never cross between airport vehicles. They may move without warning.
- Never climb on anything including trailers, trolleys, vehicles, steps or ladders unless you have been given permission and it is safe to do so.

Spotter Jotter

• Make sure you keep you possessions with you at all times.

Passenger on an Aircraft
When on board an aircraft and at an airport, please follow the points below:

• Follow the instructions of the cabin crew in relation to seat belts being fastened and the use of electronic devices. A camera does count as an electronic device and should not be switched on.
• Make sure you keep you possessions with you at all times and do not leave anything behind on the aircraft, especially your camera in the seat back pocket.

Visiting an Airport/Airfield Viewing Area
When visiting an airport/airfield visitor park, visitor centre or just at the perimeter fence, please note the following points:

• Follow and obey any signage or road markings. It is for your safety and that of the aircraft using the facility.
• Park your car in a sensible place, so as you are not blocking the traffic flow or causing an obstruction. Do not park in front of or block emergency fire gates.
• Stay back away from the edge of the kerb/road, out of the way of any passing traffic.
• Be courteous to others and don't get in the way of other members of the public who may be passing by and not share your enthusiasm for aircraft spotting.
• Be careful if using a camera monopod or tripod and not trip yourself or others up.
• Do not use flash photography. Turn your flash off.
• If challenged by authority, be polite and do what is asked.
• Walk, don't run about.
• No hi-jinx or rowdy behaviour, no matter how excited you are to get that elusive spot!
• Do not trespass to get that elusive spot or photo. It is just not worth it.
• Do not climb over, under or through a fence to get a better view.
• Do not leave any gates open.
• Make sure you keep you possessions with you at all times.
• Do not feed left over food to the birds or dispose of it on the ground.
• Take your litter home with you.

Published by Really Useful Publishing Company
Publisher's Cataloguing–in–Publication data
Jackson, Jonathan
A title of book: Aircraft Enthusiasts Spotter Jotter - 100 Page Edition / Jon Jackson

The names and/or references to any organisation, operator, manufacturer, supplier, product, service, brand etc appearing in this book are the trademarks and/or registered trademarks of their respective owners. They are used for illustrative purposes only and do not imply any endorsement, recommendation or association.

E&OE 100 Page Edition May 2016   Second Edition November 2017

ISBN–10: 153355952X   ISBN–13: 978-1533559524

Aircraft Enthusiasts

Day	Date	Month	Year

Location	

Registration	Name/Details	Operator/Details

Spotter Jotter

Day	Date	Month	Year

Location	

Registration	Name/Details	Operator/Details

Aircraft Enthusiasts

Day	Date	Month	Year

Location	

Registration	Name/Details	Operator/Details

Spotter Jotter

Day	Date	Month		Year

Location	

Registration	Name/Details	Operator/Details

Aircraft Enthusiasts

Day	Date	Month	Year

Location	

Registration	Name/Details	Operator/Details

Spotter Jotter

Day	Date	Month		Year

Location	

Registration	Name/Details	Operator/Details

Aircraft Enthusiasts

Day	Date	Month	Year

Location	

Registration	Name/Details	Operator/Details

Spotter Jotter

Day	Date	Month		Year

Location	

Registration	Name/Details	Operator/Details

Aircraft Enthusiasts

Day	Date	Month	Year

Location	

Registration	Name/Details	Operator/Details

Spotter Jotter

Day	Date	Month		Year

Location	

Registration	Name/Details	Operator/Details

Aircraft Enthusiasts

Day	Date	Month	Year

Location	

Registration	Name/Details	Operator/Details

Spotter Jotter

Day	Date	Month	Year

Location	

Registration	Name/Details	Operator/Details

Aircraft Enthusiasts

Day		Date	Month		Year

Location		

Registration	Name/Details	Operator/Details

Spotter Jotter

Day	Date	Month	Year

Location	

Registration	Name/Details	Operator/Details

Aircraft Enthusiasts

Day	Date	Month	Year

Location	

Registration	Name/Details	Operator/Details

Spotter Jotter

Day	Date	Month	Year

Location	

Registration	Name/Details	Operator/Details

Aircraft Enthusiasts

Day	Date	Month	Year

Location	

Registration	Name/Details	Operator/Details

Spotter Jotter

Day	Date	Month		Year
Location				
Registration	Name/Details		Operator/Details	

Aircraft Enthusiasts

Day	Date	Month	Year

Location	

Registration	Name/Details	Operator/Details

Spotter Jotter

Day	Date	Month		Year

Location	

Registration	Name/Details	Operator/Details

Aircraft Enthusiasts

Day	Date	Month	Year

Location	

Registration	Name/Details	Operator/Details

Spotter Jotter

Day	Date	Month	Year

Location	

Registration	Name/Details	Operator/Details

Aircraft Enthusiasts

Day	Date	Month	Year

Location	

Registration	Name/Details	Operator/Details

Spotter Jotter

Day	Date	Month		Year

Location	

Registration	Name/Details	Operator/Details

Aircraft Enthusiasts

Day	Date	Month	Year

Location	

Registration	Name/Details	Operator/Details

Spotter Jotter

Day	Date	Month		Year

Location	

Registration	Name/Details	Operator/Details

Aircraft Enthusiasts

Day	Date	Month	Year

Location	

Registration	Name/Details	Operator/Details

Spotter Jotter

Day	Date	Month		Year

Location	

Registration	Name/Details	Operator/Details

Aircraft Enthusiasts

Day	Date	Month	Year

Location	

Registration	Name/Details	Operator/Details

Spotter Jotter

Day	Date	Month		Year

Location	

Registration	Name/Details	Operator/Details

Aircraft Enthusiasts

Day	Date	Month	Year

Location	

Registration	Name/Details	Operator/Details

Spotter Jotter

Day	Date	Month		Year

Location	

Registration	Name/Details	Operator/Details

Aircraft Enthusiasts

Day	Date	Month	Year

Location	

Registration	Name/Details	Operator/Details

Spotter Jotter

Day	Date	Month	Year

Location	

Registration	Name/Details	Operator/Details

Aircraft Enthusiasts

Day	Date	Month	Year

Location	

Registration	Name/Details	Operator/Details

Spotter Jotter

Day	Date	Month	Year

Location	

Registration	Name/Details	Operator/Details

Aircraft Enthusiasts

Day	Date	Month	Year

Location	

Registration	Name/Details	Operator/Details

Spotter Jotter

Day	Date	Month	Year

Location	

Registration	Name/Details	Operator/Details

Aircraft Enthusiasts

Day	Date	Month	Year

Location	

Registration	Name/Details	Operator/Details

Spotter Jotter

Day	Date	Month		Year

Location	

Registration	Name/Details	Operator/Details

Aircraft Enthusiasts

Day	Date	Month		Year

Location	

Registration	Name/Details	Operator/Details

Spotter Jotter

Day	Date	Month		Year

Location	

Registration	Name/Details	Operator/Details

Aircraft Enthusiasts

Day	Date	Month	Year

Location	

Registration	Name/Details	Operator/Details

Spotter Jotter

Day	Date	Month		Year

Location	

Registration	Name/Details	Operator/Details

Aircraft Enthusiasts

Day	Date	Month	Year

Location	

Registration	Name/Details	Operator/Details

Spotter Jotter

Day	Date	Month	Year

Location	

Registration	Name/Details	Operator/Details

Aircraft Enthusiasts

Day	Date	Month	Year

Location	

Registration	Name/Details	Operator/Details

Spotter Jotter

Day	Date	Month		Year
Location				

Registration	Name/Details	Operator/Details

Aircraft Enthusiasts

Day	Date	Month	Year

Location	

Registration	Name/Details	Operator/Details

Spotter Jotter

Day	Date	Month	Year

Location	

Registration	Name/Details	Operator/Details

Aircraft Enthusiasts

Day	Date	Month	Year

Location	

Registration	Name/Details	Operator/Details

Spotter Jotter

Day	Date	Month		Year

Location	

Registration	Name/Details	Operator/Details

Aircraft Enthusiasts

Day	Date	Month	Year

Location	

Registration	Name/Details	Operator/Details

Spotter Jotter

Day	Date	Month		Year

Location	

Registration	Name/Details	Operator/Details

Aircraft Enthusiasts

Day	Date	Month	Year

Location	

Registration	Name/Details	Operator/Details

Spotter Jotter

Day	Date	Month		Year

Location	

Registration	Name/Details	Operator/Details

Aircraft Enthusiasts

Day	Date	Month	Year

Location	

Registration	Name/Details	Operator/Details

Spotter Jotter

Day	Date	Month	Year

Location	

Registration	Name/Details	Operator/Details

Aircraft Enthusiasts

Day	Date	Month	Year

Location	

Registration	Name/Details	Operator/Details

Spotter Jotter

Day	Date	Month		Year
Location				

Registration	Name/Details	Operator/Details

Aircraft Enthusiasts

Day	Date	Month	Year

Location		
Registration	Name/Details	Operator/Details

Spotter Jotter

Day	Date	Month	Year

Location	

Registration	Name/Details	Operator/Details

Aircraft Enthusiasts

Day	Date	Month	Year

Location	
Registration	Name/Details	Operator/Details

Spotter Jotter

Day	Date	Month	Year

Location	

Registration	Name/Details	Operator/Details

Aircraft Enthusiasts

Day	Date	Month	Year

Location	

Registration	Name/Details	Operator/Details

Spotter Jotter

Day	Date	Month		Year

Location	

Registration	Name/Details	Operator/Details

Aircraft Enthusiasts

Day	Date	Month	Year

Location	

Registration	Name/Details	Operator/Details

Spotter Jotter

Day	Date	Month		Year

Location	

Registration	Name/Details	Operator/Details

Aircraft Enthusiasts

Day	Date	Month	Year

Location	

Registration	Name/Details	Operator/Details

Spotter Jotter

Day	Date	Month	Year

Location	

Registration	Name/Details	Operator/Details

Aircraft Enthusiasts

Day	Date	Month	Year

Location	

Registration	Name/Details	Operator/Details

Spotter Jotter

Day	Date	Month	Year

Location	

Registration	Name/Details	Operator/Details

Aircraft Enthusiasts

Day	Date	Month		Year

Location	

Registration	Name/Details	Operator/Details

Spotter Jotter

Day	Date	Month	Year

Location	

Registration	Name/Details	Operator/Details

Aircraft Enthusiasts

Day	Date	Month	Year

Location	
Registration	Name/Details	Operator/Details

Spotter Jotter

Day	Date	Month	Year

Location	

Registration	Name/Details	Operator/Details

Aircraft Enthusiasts

Day	Date	Month	Year

Location	

Registration	Name/Details	Operator/Details

Spotter Jotter

Day	Date	Month		Year

Location	

Registration	Name/Details	Operator/Details

Aircraft Enthusiasts

Day	Date	Month		Year

Location	

Registration	Name/Details	Operator/Details

Spotter Jotter

Day	Date	Month	Year

Location	

Registration	Name/Details	Operator/Details

Aircraft Enthusiasts

Day	Date	Month	Year

Location	

Registration	Name/Details	Operator/Details

Spotter Jotter

Day	Date	Month	Year

Location	

Registration	Name/Details	Operator/Details

Aircraft Enthusiasts

Day	Date	Month	Year

Location	

Registration	Name/Details	Operator/Details

Spotter Jotter

Day	Date	Month	Year

Location	

Registration	Name/Details	Operator/Details

Aircraft Enthusiasts

Day	Date	Month	Year

Location	
Registration	Name/Details	Operator/Details

Spotter Jotter

Day	Date	Month	Year

Location	

Registration	Name/Details	Operator/Details

Aircraft Enthusiasts

Day	Date	Month	Year

Location	

Registration	Name/Details	Operator/Details

Spotter Jotter

Day	Date	Month	Year

Location	

Registration	Name/Details	Operator/Details

Aircraft Enthusiasts

Day	Date	Month	Year

Location	

Registration	Name/Details	Operator/Details

Spotter Jotter

Day	Date	Month		Year

Location	

Registration	Name/Details	Operator/Details

Aircraft Enthusiasts

Day	Date	Month	Year

Location	

Registration	Name/Details	Operator/Details

Spotter Jotter

Day	Date	Month		Year
Location				
Registration	Name/Details		Operator/Details	

Aircraft Enthusiasts

Day	Date	Month	Year

Location	

Registration	Name/Details	Operator/Details

Spotter Jotter

Day	Date	Month	Year

Location	

Registration	Name/Details	Operator/Details

Aircraft Enthusiasts

Day	Date	Month	Year

Location	

Registration	Name/Details	Operator/Details

Spotter Jotter

Day	Date	Month	Year

Location	

Registration	Name/Details	Operator/Details

Aircraft Enthusiasts

Day	Date	Month	Year

Location	

Registration	Name/Details	Operator/Details

Another Really Useful book...

OPEN SESAME
Password Vault

Cliff Bretford

Nowadays, you need a password for just about everything you can think of - mobile phone, computer, Wi-Fi, email, social media and banking to name but a few. So unless you have a phenomenal memory for remembering passwords and other associated security details you will no doubt already be writing down your passwords or password prompts anyway, probably on scraps of paper or storing passwords in your email account

So instead of doing either of these, you can now write your password details down in this easy to use book. Disguised as a novel and containing some useful password tips, it has been clearly laid out in alphabetical order for ease of access, allowing you to record all your various security details.

Available now from good book sellers

ISBN–13: 978-1540443274

Also available for enthusiasts...

Safety and Security
Be Alert - Remain Vigilant

If you See Something, Say Something.
If you see anything suspicious, or an unlocked gate or broken/danaged fence, please report it to a member of staff or the Police immediately. If you believe you have spotted something suspicious, remember the HOT principles:

Hidden?
Has any attempt been made to conceal the item from view or place it where accidental discovery is unlikely? Innocent items are not usually hidden deliberately. Explosive devices are not usually left in the open.

Obviously Suspicious?
Does it look like an explosive device? Does it have wiring, circuitry, a power supply or something that may appear to be explosives attached to it? Has it been found after a suspicious event?

Typical of the Environment?
Is the item typical of what you might reasonably expect to find in that location? For example, lost property is often found in locations where people congregate or wait before moving to a new location?

If you report the suspicious item to the police, make a note of the following:

- **WHAT** is it? What does it look like?
- **WHERE** is it? What is the best means of approach? Are there any obstacles or nearby hazards?
- **WHEN** was it found? Do you know when it wasn't there? Has it been moved since it was found?
- **WHY** is it suspicious? What parts of the HOT protocol makes you think it is suspicious?
- **WHO** has seen it? Keep any witnesses available so they can report what they saw.

Report any suspicious activity by calling the Police on:

- **999** (UK), **112** (Europe/mobile), **911** (North America)

Other emergency services including Fire and Ambulance can also be contacted on:

- **999** (UK), **112** (Europe/mobile), **911** (North America)

The UK Police can also be contacted on **101** for non emergency calls.

Made in the USA
Middletown, DE
06 May 2018